Down Anstruther Way

TOBI ALFIER

FUTURECYCLE PRESS
www.futurecycle.org

Photographs: "Down Anstruther Way," "Pigeons on a Rail Bridge, Paisley, Scotland," and "Abandoned Boat on the Isle of Mull Road"

Copyright © 2016 Jeffrey C. Alfier

Copyright © 2016 Tobi Alfier
All Rights Reserved

Published by FutureCycle Press
Lexington, Kentucky, USA

ISBN 978-1-942371-20-5

Jeff, all that I am is dedicated to you

Contents

Beginnings 9
Evening in Oban 10
Cello 11
Young Piper and the Large Silver Bus 12
On the Road to a Day Trip on Iona 14
Excursion Out of Loch Shiel and Mingarry Park 15
His Turn 16
In the Silence of our Weariness 17
Springtime in Perthshire 18
Inland from Kinloss 19
Inverness Portside Blues 20
The Photographer Loosens Up a Bit, Documents Paisley Town 22
Photo Assignment in Fort William 24
Down Anstruther Way 25
One Worn Man in Anyone's Harbor Town 26
The Color of Ashes 27
Trawler of the Northern Lights 28
Mull to Ulva 30
Waulking the Tweed 31
Gypsy Aubade 32
Coda 33

Down Anstruther Way

Beginnings

Don't start with the dawn;
start with the rise of the moon
as it lights snow on mountains and an audience
of clouds, all so bright your way is lit
without lantern or tired streetlight glow.

Don't start with your first sight of each other
across a packed dance floor, fingers snapping
to match the bass of the band; start with coming
to conscious wakefulness that first morning
after you marry—you twist your rings, pinch

yourself to make sure you're not dreaming.
His arm wrapped around your waist, knees
tucked up into the bench of your bent legs,
his breath warming the back of your neck—
thus begins the next thirty, forty, fifty years.

Don't start with the common car park; wander
through moors and magic, past waterfalls, dreamers
and dusty roads, exposed peat, nested ledges,
past cottages, past memories long and lasting.
Don't start with the hunt; start with the rescue.

Evening in Oban

A table for sitting,
the profile of your strong jaw
as you scan the horizon
for boats and wayfarers.
A rooftop chapel of silence
but for the outside flutes
of wind brushing leaves,
birds heading home,
and the crinkle of water
along the shoreline
as ferries slowly cruise to sleep
until beginning again with the sun.
Forested ruins spotlit by stars
and us, holding hands,
a bottle of red and one of water
between us, our blended
observations deliberately low,
as an audience will whisper
while leaning toward the orchestra,
waiting for those first real notes
of night.

Cello

She is reflected backwards
in the shadow box of mirrors,
her head nodding to the beat.
A Scottish love ballad,
fine and keening. Her toes
naked under the lace of her long
dress tap on the Astroturf
under the folding chair from
Smart & Final—an ordinary
reddish-slate chair, cold
to the touch.
She does not have time to eat,
her exercise the hours of playing
beautiful and solitary music.
No matter if hundreds listen or
no one listens. She plays
the cello; she was too feminine
to play the bass. She sweeps her
hair back and pins it up. She
sometimes plays with her
eyes closed. She is always
smiling, even when her feet
are cold against the winter
floor. Her love songs and laments
are calling. Please buy her music.

Young Piper and the Large Silver Bus

Not all young men stay a part of farm
or fisherboat, lives ordained by obligation

or history handed down. For some that world's
far too small, so off they go. They leave their wellies

by home in case they're needed, but dad
and the brothers have it all sorted out—

by tide and weather, little red markers,
a new creel winch—Angus is cut loose and free.

Angus drives the bus and plays the pipes.
When waiting for his charges, he memorizes

new tunes, committing to memory
something for his gig next Saturday

when Betty will be there to listen,
toe-tapping, eyes only for him.

Come with us, they say, *please come.*
Take the whisky tour, just don't drink.

He'd rather raise up his seat, quietly shush
the beats so no one hears,

or go outside to "properly" wash the tires—
in the rain—to shush a bit louder,

keep his arms and breath in right firm order
for playing. It's a good life. Home once a month

for church and catch-up, a pocket of tip-cash
at week's end, a gig, a girl, music flaring in the wind.

On the Road to a Day Trip on Iona

Yesterday Irene sat in her doorway,
freshly curled from the beauty parlor,
pale green slacks, white sweater.
She would wear gloves if she could.
She is protected from a cool breeze,
another sweater across her shoulders.

There she sits in a lawn chair blocking
her entryway, wearing the serene smile
of a music teacher listening to her prize student.
Her head metronomes left to right
as she watches the busses, campers with bicycles,
and tourists go by on the way to the ferry.

She herself has a voice so beautiful
it is also music, but there is no one to hear.
She has been widowed forever.
Westering light moves through altered shapes
of silence. The last of the cars ghosts toward home.

Excursion Out of Loch Shiel and Mingarry Park

And gingerly he steps among the rocks along the stream,
perfect S-turns winding through a green, green valley
dotted with sheep. Sheep along the road above him
graze as they please; some promenade straight down
the center of the narrow one-lane, cars in either direction
echoing the turns and twists of the water below. Drivers are
alert, patient, respectful of the animals belonging to many crofts
and to this valley.

A song plays inside his head to help him balance.
His arms free to teeter him from stone to stone,
he is a grounded aerialist, almost crossed and looking
for a place to rest.

He will lunch on whatever Emma folded into his pack—
he had left as light began to make a tiered layering of dark clouds,
muted sun dotted with the tops of hills, and green below.
She'd handed him a pack. *To keep your arms free,* she'd said.
Fergie, bed-headed and hung over, was hunched over a steaming
cup in the kitchen. He'd straightened up to wish him
good adventures and *see-you-soon.*

Our traveler guesses from the powdered-sugar handprint
on Fergie's black pants that at least one jammy shortcake
awaits his dessert. He is impatient, anticipatory, hungry.
He has crossed the stream and found a lovely dry spot.
With warmth on his face and the gentle reflection
off the breeze-murmured waters on the Loch in the distance,
he sits...

His Turn

In his hotel, a tired woman with his same view
looks out before a short lie-down.
Listening to pipes played below,
they both watch a ship slowly angle toward a breach
between two hills across the bay.

Sky, mist, water and ship are a lovely mind-photo;
the song of pipes wishing safe travels
adds an aural effect to this tableau.

A smaller ferry and two rotting workshops stay fast
against the dock. Street-level conversation and traffic
remind him this is not a dream.

Flags fly. Radar antennas whirl like whisks
in a bowl of creamy cloud. Now he understands
what it is to watch, to listen, to hear in his heart
the sound of waiting.

In the Silence of our Weariness

Moonlight came fractured
through the hotel skylight
and through the stripes,
wide as shutter-slats,
I watched you dream.

Your breath calm and shining
in cool air fanned
by one small window—
open for fresh air
and the smells of the season.

One hand under your cheek,
the other holding mine,
a magic hour until I too
joined your dreams,
woke to birdsong and violets,
a filigree of light—
a day like no other.

Springtime in Perthshire

Soft vibrations in a field of grass,
bladed and poppied. The rhythmic

chug of a cargo train crosses
left to right, a distance away.

His shoes come off.
He recalls a sundown journey

in a life too far off to regather.
Three white horses, patient

and pale as childhood unicorns,
share their field as he lies down.

Popcorn clouds are white, parceled
through the clear and quiet sky.

He closes his eyes, his mind clear
as the breeze washing over him.

A lifetime of mercy summoned
in a few brief minutes.

Spikes of green caress his palms—
laid flat, warming, released.

Inland from Kinloss

                        And oh those back roads,
wearied ballads of rust and small white flowers,
the far-off bark of some fisherman's dog
chasing a teasing cat, both blooming in the sun,
resting in shade, waiting for the master to come
home with his catch and the key to the gate.

A young girl picks carefully over railroad sleepers,
green flourishing between. Her boots place her square,
shorts place her *I am still a child, not quite yet a woman,*
long straight hair and the folk song she hums along her way
complete this scene of artless beauty. Traffic

is on main roads in another time, where families
don't know the history of their neighbors,
and a pint shared makes you nobody's friend.
Back roads with trees weeping shade, a barrel
placed nowhere for a brief sit, where a traveler
scrawls a few notes for memory before moving on.

This gift from the land to the witness climbs
in and burrows like comfort. It will stay with you
always, if you allow. A secret, just like the name
of the road, unmarked until you happen upon
a small sign, a garland, and knowing this is yours.

Inverness Portside Blues

I

Crows plague this street.
They startle us from out of the trees,
from rooftops, the dead branches
of palms. As each morning rises
they start, do not stop till the sun
flashes green over the horizon
and falls into the sea.

II

They appear and disappear, shadows
dragging trash and squirming lawn-fauna
like the gypsy knife grinder drags
his wagon—up driveways, over ruts
and cracks, to have tea with the ladies,
whisky with the gents. He sharpens
it all. John next door has a criss-cross
shredder; the cost of sharpening
is a full bottle of Jack, a Coke chaser,
and a story about anything other

than this street, this town, where Moses
from down pierway drives a '58 pickup
with column shift—a city auction relic—
to pick up scrap, sell it for dimes,
buy the right to light a candle
on Sundays and call his life good.

III

He makes more charging folks
three bucks to take a picture
but he doesn't care—when he hears
those damn crows at dawn,
it's his time to shine, to uncoil
from night's half-sleep. With a sandwich,
a plaid thermos and his route, he waves
to us, waves to the knife grinder,
keeps watch on the crows.
Another day, back-breaking,
trash-talking, spare change
and a smile.

The Photographer Loosens Up a Bit, Documents Paisley Town

Two pigeons calmly watch it all.
Even when they move from place to place,
they are as quiet as the lovely green
that spruces between crags in stone,

in underpasses, in buildings mottled
with character and the characters within,
boarded-up backgrounds and these two,
dovelike and fragile, memorizing the lesson
that towns don't always die, no matter

their look. Here there is still the charisma
and charm of a wee nip a bit early
at the Wee Barrel. Its two regulars
have been married so long they share
laugh lines; they come out into the street

so the anonymous photographer,
soon to be having his own pint or two
at Wellington Bar, can take their picture,
adjust it to grayscale, look back
with nostalgia.

The pigeons, on their current perch,
await their turn to be noticed and captured
into history. Their calm is echoed by nearby
ancient graves sinking next to an abbey,
also off-plumb.

The venue changes. Still vigilant, our birds
document the now slightly less anonymous
photographer as he takes cheer in Balingowan Arms,
sings a chorus under his breath with the barmaid.

A Belhaven, "balanced and honey colored,"
compliments the outdoor cobbles and moss,
the red of a train trellis, brick of the station.
A town of wonder. Of laughter and music.
Silent wings. Silent witness.

Pigeons on a Rail Bridge, Paisley, Scotland

Photo Assignment in Fort William

He has many photographs of women gazing.
Young women leaning out third-floor windows,
modest cleavage over the sill, they watch,
expressions of joyous contemplation
or thoughtful listening across their brows.

One woman waits for the sound of her love
coming round the corner, swinging
his lunchpail with the tiredness of end-of-day.
When he looks up she will burst onto him,
a smile lit from within, all the suns
in the universe welcoming him home.

A nighttime wait is quite another expression.
As he sings himself home from the pub,
she watches the traffic around him, prays
for his safe up-the-stairs, prays harder
that all she'll detect is the scent of lager
and tobacco, his neck unstained
by the color of anyone else's smile.

Down Anstruther Way

It is summer.
A small crowd rides a crest of laughter
propelled by somebody's radio,
the speakers turned up and out,
a rousing ballad.

He has drunk whisky
to this song, broad smile, arms clasped
upon the shoulders of fellow neighbors
with a love for the farm and knack
for turning rocky quadrants into lettuces
and leeks.

He has hunched deeply over this song,
head foggy with a wall of sadness.
Remembering the fleeting dusk,
her woolen cloak disappearing round
the corner, the note not yet
discovered, the silvering moon.

He knows the land
but not the woman. He knows
the skies and the vanishing tides,
the brief grace between storms,
the familiar gait of his boy
as he ambles toward home.

The sun finds its place deep in the west,
an outdoor cathedral as light bursts
onto the wet stone of uneven village roads.
The radio changes to a dream;
a young girl starts to dance.

One Worn Man in Anyone's Harbor Town

Weary as the granite sky,
where the jagged edge of storms
turns clouds to pale and dark,
a vision you know by a heart
that could be the same as yours.

Silent as a cautionary sea,
and sad, a slow surrender
as you walk to your lonely rooms,
aged and tired, past doors
where marriages succeeded,
to a bottle and a bathroom glass.

You read the word *slattern,*
know it is your graceless landlady.
A ring of keys the only music
in this raw season of unhappiness,
surely the freeze before the thaw,
the late moon trying to help you
find your way home.

The Color of Ashes

The soap factory, vacant in morning light.
Not a soul but the watchman dozing
in dreamless, coffee-restless sleep.

A Far East container ship in port, buoyed
and anchored, the water line a demarcation
of a full hold. Only the rust-copper of rail cars

different from the absent, quiet sea.
A woman picking up empties
in the parking lot of last night's bar,

gravel turning over, masking the dirt
underneath; she quietly hums plaintive blues
into morning's luck while her only son

dreams at home, curled around an old
stuffed bear, hoping mum brings porridge
home for breakfast, and hot for once.

There is no word in Japanese for gray.
They say it's the color of ashes,
the color of a working man's hymn.

Trawler of the Northern Lights

There's something about a love letter
delivered by the mail boat's semiweekly run.

First off-loaded are haddock and cod—some flash-
frozen miles offshore, some faltering in creels and traps.

Lobster, their tendrils winding through
the metal mesh like leaves tenderly climbing a trellis,

heaved up on deck by men in rain slickers
over thick wool sweaters knitted by wives—

home, by fireplaces, accustomed
to being alone while their men bring a piece

of their lives to the counties of Northern Lights
and endless darkness. Next off-loaded,

the hardware. Boxes of screws, beams,
parts for cars once driven by our grandparents,

cars that found their way north,
drivable only a few weeks each year

when the snow melts, ancient tracks uncovered
and dried in weak sun. Then medical supplies,

always needed, newspapers now weeks old,
books read by the crew and exchanged for the ones

from last trip and, finally, the mail. Soggy, fragile,
stinking of fish but never unwelcome,

a reminder of patience, mottled with raindrops
posing as tears, a checkmark on the calendar.

You will be together soon. Soon enough.
The boat of the bringer will take you home.

Mull to Ulva

Because the distance from land-shore to island
is a finger snap in the constant of all time.

Because the tides bless fishermen and landlocked alike,
full creels the harvest here, no watery graves, no tears.

Because the store displays bait and boat, strong needles
for sewing the lace of fishing line, not delicate woman-lace.

Because the sun burns with savage brightness, much
as the evening stars will burn unwatched and unwished upon.

Because the ghosts of old souls and older relics own
the dark, with nary a mortal light upon any land, sea or shore.

Because here, no one interprets the thousand pinpricks
composing a symphony in the edgy blackness of night.

Because the fragrance of this summer conjures
memory after memory of all pasts and futures.

Because there is no caretaker, no guardian to aid thin fog
searching the inlet for crevice with which to gain purchase—

I wish to walk barefoot on old stone, become one
with the earth and sea, learn their secrets,

raise my arms to the stars.
Palm to palm, our hearts.

Waulking the Tweed

I remember when it was our mum's turn—
she bustled with energy as she waited

for the other farm ladies
to assemble after breakfast,

her apron clean, not a crease,
food and drink on the side for later,

for pauses in the back-breaking day.
A bit of whisky as the end neared.

Faces shone with sweat;
eyes sparkled with exhilaration

as if the statues in church spoke
and spoke only to them.

Voices hoarse from the songs passed down
and down, one day passed to me,

now only for demonstration—
everything's mechanized these days.

No finger crook, no clapping song,
no rolling the tweed tight, pulling it soft;

no catching up on croft news, town news
family news, happy, aching as sore arms—

fingers and songs marked the setting sun;
another day was done.

Gypsy Aubade

We lean in the tide of scented moonlight,
two travelers selling themselves for the sea.
Night winds howl in doorways but we—
who are blessed,
hear not the high pitched cries but the alto
undertones of rain-washed thunder.

The skies have already bid goodbye to winter.

This one last turn of the roulette wheel,
a carnival stopping at dawnlight and amber—there
will be no more rain until the calendar advances many
fully lit night skies. We are safe, gripping woolens
wrapped tightly, our gloves fingerless
so we can touch gently.

Fingers sieve weeds
growing in quayside cracks while our
other hands grip the pulse and heartbeat of each other.
A dulcimer song, a drum, the crest of eye-crinkles
and loving laughter. A sharp breath inhaled.

What rises from behind the hill that's
more than this? A palomino in a field of thistle
stamps one foot and tells us night has drifted away.
The selfish sea cares not, signals grandly
and without remorse that it's time to go.

Coda

She saw many a boat, some on the Lochs, some resting in the wet mud of outbound tide, some ruined and unworthy of any water, green growing up through cracks in the wood, beautiful and forlorn, a family's livelihood reduced to flowering hulls and photographs taken by passing travelers. She rode the ferry, rain stinging her eyes like a thousand razors, cold biting through to her bones, counting the seconds to minutes to hearing the loudspeaker-voice, feeling the chunk of steel upon pier, walking to cover and warmth. She watched many a layer of cloud darken sun, sky and sea, bruised purple and angry, the definition of roiling and silent, a sullen topping of hills wishing to be green, reduced to angry gray. She never noticed any clear sky—it was always held hostage by mist. All she wanted was to make a wish. She looked down for beauty; she wished on the tiny white flowers beside the road, pretended they were stars.

Abandoned Boat on the Isle of Mull Road

Acknowledgments

Grateful acknowledgment is made to the following journals, in which these poems originally appeared, or are forthcoming, sometimes in slightly different form:

Bellowing Ark: "Cello"
Broadkill Review: "Inland from Kinloss," "Mull to Ulva," "Waulking the Tweed"
Dead Mule School of Southern Literature: "His Turn," "Springtime in Perthshire"
Gravel Magazine: "The Color of Ashes"
Illya's Honey: "Excursion Out of Loch Shiel and Mingarry Park"
JuxtaProse Literary Magazine: "One Worn Man in Anyone's Harbor Town"
Poetry Salzburg Review: "Trawler of the Northern Lights"
Red River Review: "Beginnings," "Young Piper and the Large Silver Bus"
Skylight 47 (Ire): "Trawler of the Northern Lights"
Suisun Valley Review: "Coda"
The Galway Review (Ire): "Evening in Oban," "Photo Assignment in Fort William"
The Northridge Review: "Gypsy Aubade"
The Roaring Muse: "Down Anstruther Way"

All photographs by Jeffrey C. Alfier
Copyright © 2016. Used with permission.

Cover photo, author photo, and interior photos by Jeffrey C. Alfier; cover and interior book design by Diane Kistner; Georgia text and Foglihten PCS titling

About FutureCycle Press

FutureCycle Press is dedicated to publishing lasting English-language poetry books, chapbooks, and anthologies in both print-on-demand and Kindle ebook formats. Founded in 2007 by long-time independent editor/publishers and partners Diane Kistner and Robert S. King, the press incorporated as a nonprofit in 2012. A number of our editors are distinguished poets and writers in their own right, and we have been actively involved in the small press movement going back to the early seventies.

The FutureCycle Poetry Book Prize and honorarium is awarded annually for the best full-length volume of poetry we publish in a calendar year. Introduced in 2013, our Good Works projects are anthologies devoted to issues of universal significance, with all proceeds donated to a related worthy cause. Our Selected Poems series highlights contemporary poets with a substantial body of work to their credit; with this series we strive to resurrect work that has had limited distribution and is now out of print.

We are dedicated to giving all of the authors we publish the care their work deserves, making our catalog of titles the most diverse and distinguished it can be, and paying forward any earnings to fund more great books.

We've learned a few things about independent publishing over the years. We've also evolved a unique, resilient publishing model that allows us to focus mainly on vetting and preserving for posterity poetry collections of exceptional quality without becoming overwhelmed with bookkeeping and mailing, fundraising activities, or taxing editorial and production "bubbles." To find out more about what we are doing, come see us at www.futurecycle.org.

www.ingramcontent.com/pod-product-compliance
Lightning Source LLC
Chambersburg PA
CBHW070454050426
42450CB00012B/3273